Harold Pinter was born in London in 1930. He is married to Antonia Fraser.

HAROLD PINTER

The Hothouse

faber and faber

LONDON · BOSTON

First published in 1980 by Eyre Methuen Ltd
Revised paperback edition published in 1982
by Methuen London Ltd
This paperback edition first published in 1991
by Faber and Faber Limited
3 Queen Square London WCIN 3AU

Printed in England by Clays Ltd, St Ives plc

All rights whatsoever in this play are strictly reserved and
applications to perform, etc., should be made in writing, before
rehearsals begin, to Judy Daish Associates, 83 Eastbourne Mews,
London W2 6LQ.

A CIP record for this book is available
from the British Library

ISBN 0-571-16086-7

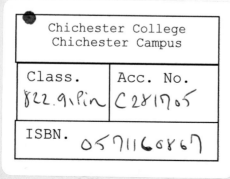

To Henry Woolf

Author's Note

I wrote *The Hothouse* in the winter of 1958. I put it aside for further deliberation and made no attempt to have it produced at the time. I then went on to write *The Caretaker*. In 1979 I re-read *The Hothouse* and decided it was worth presenting on the stage. I made a few changes during rehearsal, mainly cuts.

HAROLD PINTER

Characters

ROOTE, *in his fifties*

GIBBS, *in his thirties*

LAMB, *in his twenties*

MISS CUTTS, *in her thirties*

LUSH, *in his thirties*

TUBB, *fifty*

LOBB, *fifty*

The Hothouse was first presented at Hampstead Theatre, London, on 24 April 1980 in a production directed by Harold Pinter. It moved to the Ambassador Theatre, London, on 25 June 1980.

The cast was as follows:

ROOTE	Derek Newark
GIBBS	James Grant
LAMB	Roger Davidson
MISS CUTTS	Angela Pleasence
LUSH	Robert East
TUBB	Michael Forrest
LOBB	Edward de Souza

Director Harold Pinter
Designer Eileen Diss

Locations

ROOTE's *office*
A stairway
A sitting room
A soundproof room
LOBB's *office in the Ministry*

Act One

ROOTE's *office. Morning.*
ROOTE *is standing at the window, looking out.*
GIBBS *is at the filing cabinet, examining some papers.*

ROOTE

Gibbs.

GIBBS

Yes, sir?

ROOTE

Tell me . . .

GIBBS

Yes, sir?

ROOTE

How's 6457 getting on?

GIBBS

6457, sir?

ROOTE

Yes.

GIBBS

He's dead, sir.

ROOTE

Dead?

GIBBS

He died on Thursday, sir.

ROOTE

Thursday? What are you talking about? What's today?

GIBBS

Saturday, sir.

ROOTE

Saturday . . . Well, for goodness sake, I had a talk with him, when was it? (*Opens his desk diary.*) Recently. Only the other day. Yesterday, I think. Just a minute.

GIBBS

I hardly think yesterday, sir.

ROOTE

Why not?

GIBBS

I supervised the burial arrangements myself, sir.

ROOTE

This is ridiculous. What did he die of?

GIBBS

I beg your pardon, sir?

ROOTE

If he's dead, what did he die of?

GIBBS

Heart failure, sir.

ROOTE *stares at him, sits at the desk and consults the diary.*

ROOTE

Wait . . . here we are. Got it. Conversation with 6457 ten o'clock Friday morning. That was yesterday. Well, what do you make of that?

GIBBS

I'm afraid there seems to be a slight discrepancy, sir.

ROOTE

Discrepancy! I'm damn sure there's a discrepancy! You come and tell me that a man has died and I've got it down here that I had a conversation with him yesterday morning. According to you he was in his grave. There does seem to be a slight discrepancy, I agree with you.

GIBBS

I meant . . . about the dates, sir.

ROOTE

Dates? What dates?

GIBBS

In your diary, sir. (*He moves to the desk.*) I must point out that you are in fact referring to Friday, the 17th. (*He indicates a date on the page.*) There, sir. Yesterday was Friday the 24th. (*He turns the pages forward and indicates a date.*) Here, sir. You had a conversation with 6457 on the 17th. He died on the 23rd. (*Indicates a date.*) Here.

ROOTE

What! (*He turns the pages back.*) Good Lord, you're right. You're quite right. How extraordinary. I haven't written a single thing down in this diary for a whole week.

GIBBS

You've held no interviews with any of the patients, sir, during the last week.

ROOTE

No, I haven't, have I? Why not?

GIBBS

You decided on the ... 18th, sir, that you would cancel all interviews until further notice.

ROOTE (*slowly*)

Oh yes. So I did.

GIBBS *moves round the desk.*

GIBBS

For the sake of accuracy, sir, I'd like, if I may, to point out to you what is apparently another discrepancy.

ROOTE

Another one?

GIBBS

Yes, sir.

ROOTE

You're very keen this morning, aren't you, Gibbs?

GIBBS

I do try to keep my powers of observation well exercised, sir.

ROOTE

Don't stand so close to me. You're right on top of me. What's the matter with you?

GIBBS

I'm so sorry, sir. (*He steps away from the desk.*)

ROOTE

There's plenty of room in here, isn't there? What are you breathing down my neck for?

GIBBS

I do apologise, sir.

ROOTE

Nothing's more irritating.

GIBBS

It was thoughtless of me, sir.

Pause

ROOTE

Well . . . what was this *other* discrepancy, anyway?

GIBBS (*flatly*)

It was not 6457, sir, whom you interviewed on the 17th.

ROOTE

Gibbs.

GIBBS

Sir?

ROOTE

One question.

GIBBS

Sir.

ROOTE

Are you taking the piss out of me?

GIBBS

Most decidedly not, sir.

Slight pause

ROOTE

All right. You have just said it was not 6457 I interviewed on the 17th. What evidence have you got to support your contention?

GIBBS

The figures in your diary, sir.

ROOTE

Figures?

GIBBS

One figure, sir. If I may . . . (*He bends over the desk.*) . . . this one.

ROOTE

Which one?

GIBBS

This one. It's not a seven, sir. It's a nine.

ROOTE

Nine?

GIBBS

Nine, sir. The number is 645 . . . 9.

ROOTE

Good God, so it is. Nine. Well, it's not a very clear nine, is it?

GIBBS

It was in fact 6459 whom you interviewed, sir.

ROOTE

Must have been. That's funny. I wonder why I thought it was seven. (*He rises abruptly.*) The whole thing's ridiculous! The system's wrong. (*He walks across the room.*) We shouldn't use these stupid numbers at all. Only confuses things. Why don't we use their names, for God's sake? They've got names, haven't they?

GIBBS

It was your predecessor who instituted the use of numbers, sir.

ROOTE

How do you know?

GIBBS

So I understand, sir.

ROOTE

You weren't even here then.

GIBBS

No, sir.

ROOTE

I was.

GIBBS

Quite, sir.

ROOTE

I was standing where you're standing now. I can tell you that. Saying yes sir, no sir and certainly sir. Just as you are now. I didn't bribe anyone to get where I am. I worked my way up. When my predecessor ... retired ... I was invited to take over his position. And have you any idea why you call me sir now?

GIBBS

Yes, sir.

ROOTE

Why?

GIBBS

Because you called him sir then, sir.

Right!

Pause

But I sometimes think I've been a bit slow in making changes. Change is the order of things, after all. I mean it's *in* the order of things, it's not *the* order of things, it's *in* the order of things.

Slight pause

Still, I sometimes think I could have instituted a few more changes — if I'd had time. I'm not talking about many changes or drastic changes. That's not necessary. But on this numbers business, for instance. It would make things so much simpler if we called them by their names. Then we'd all know where we were. After all, they're not criminals. They're only people in need of help, which we try to give, in one way or another, to the best of our discretion, to the best of our judgement, to help them regain their confidence, confidence in themselves, confidence in others, confidence in . . . the world. What? They're all people specially recommended by the Ministry, after all. They're not any Tom, Dick or . . . or . . . er . . . Harry.

He stops, brooding.

I often think it must depress them . . . somewhat . . . to have a number rapped at them all the time. After some of them have been here a few years they're liable to forget what names their fathers gave them. Or their mothers.

Pause

One of the purposes of this establishment is to instill that confidence in each and every one of them, that confidence which will one day enable them to say 'I am . . . Gubbins', for example. Not easy, not easy, agreed, but it makes it doubly difficult if they're constantly referred to as 5244, doesn't it? We lose sight of their names and they lose sight of their names. I sometimes wonder if it's the right way to go about things. (*He sits at the desk.*)

GIBBS

Would you like me to place further consideration of this matter on the agenda, sir?

ROOTE (*sharply*)

Certainly not. We can't.

GIBBS

Can't, sir?

ROOTE

You know damn well we can't. That was one of the rules of procedure laid down in the original constitution. The patients are to be given numbers and called by those numbers. And that's how it's got to remain. You understand?

GIBBS

Perfectly, sir.

GIBBS *goes to the filing cabinet.*

ROOTE

A death on the premises?

GIBBS

Sir?

ROOTE

A death? You say this man has died?

GIBBS

6457, sir? Yes, sir.

ROOTE

Which one was he?

GIBBS

You had quite a lot to do with him, actually, sir.

ROOTE

He was a man I dealt with personally?

GIBBS

Yes, sir.

ROOTE

Well, which one was he, for God's sake?

GIBBS

You knew him well, sir.

ROOTE

You keep saying that! But I can't remember a damn thing about him. What did he look like?

Pause

GIBBS

Thinnish.

ROOTE

Fairheaded?

GIBBS (*sitting*)

Not darkheaded, sir.

Pause

ROOTE

Tall?

GIBBS

Certainly not small.

Pause

ROOTE

Quite a sharp sort of face?

GIBBS

Quite sharp, yes, sir.

ROOTE

Yes.

Pause

Yes, he had a sharp sort of face, didn't he?

GIBBS

I should say it was sharp, sir, yes.

ROOTE

Limped a bit?

GIBBS

Oh, possibly a trifle, sir.

ROOTE

Yes, he limped. He limped on his left leg.

GIBBS

His left, sir?

ROOTE

Well, one of them. I'm sure of it.

GIBBS

Yes, he had a slight limp, sir.

ROOTE

Yes, of course he had.

Pause

He had a slight limp. Whenever he walked anywhere . . . he limped. Prematurely grey, he was. Prematurely grey.

Pause

Yes, I remember him very well.

Pause

He's dead, you say?

GIBBS

Yes, sir.

ROOTE

Then why wasn't I told? It's your job to keep me informed of all developments in this building, no matter how slight, no matter how trivial. I demand an answer. Why wasn't I told?

GIBBS

You signed the death certificate, sir.

GIBBS *goes to the filing cabinet.*

ROOTE

Did he get a decent burial?

GIBBS

Oh, very decent, sir.

ROOTE

I don't see why I wasn't invited. Who said the last words over him?

GIBBS

There were no last words, sir.

ROOTE (*appalled*)

No last words?

ROOTE *rises, walks to the window, looks out.*

Snowing. Isn't it the patients' exercise time?

GIBBS

Not today, sir.

ROOTE

Why not?

GIBBS

It's Christmas day, sir.

ROOTE *goes back to the desk and sits.*

ROOTE
All right, that's all for now. Bear everything in mind.

He examines some papers. GIBBS *does not move.* ROOTE *looks up.*

What is it? What are you waiting for?

GIBBS
You asked me a question earlier, sir, which I haven't yet had a chance to answer.

ROOTE
Haven't had a chance? What do you mean? That I've been talking too much or something?

GIBBS
Not at all, sir. We simply passed on to another topic.

ROOTE (*regarding him*)
Gibbs.

GIBBS
Sir?

ROOTE (*confidentially*)
Between ourselves, man to man, you're not by any chance taking the old wee-wee out of me, are you?

GIBBS
Most assuredly not, sir. By no means. I merely feel it incumbent upon me to answer any questions you put to me, or to do

my best to do so. You are dependent upon me for certain information and I feel it in the line of duty to supply you with it, especially when it is by specific request.

ROOTE

Stop mouthing! This has been a most exhausting morning. If the morning's like this what's the rest of the day going to be like? There's no system, that's the trouble. Look. The next time I ask you a question answer it and we won't waste so much time fiddling about. Things are getting much too slack around here.

Pause

Well, come on, what was this question?

GIBBS

You asked me, sir –

ROOTE

Wait!

He leans forward on the desk.

(*Quietly.*) Before you go on, Gibbs, let me say one thing. Be sure that what you say is accurate. You are about to quote a question you say I put to you. I don't know what you're going to say, but immediately you've said it I shall know whether I said it, or whether I didn't. I shall know.

GIBBS

Yes, sir.

ROOTE

I didn't get this job for nothing, I can assure you. I shall
know. Have no doubt whatsoever on that point.

GIBBS

No, sir.

ROOTE

Stick to the facts, man, and we won't go far wrong.

GIBBS

Yes, sir.

Pause

ROOTE

Well, what was this question?

GIBBS

You asked me how 6459 was getting on, sir.

Pause

ROOTE (*expressionless*)

Did I?

GIBBS

To be quite accurate, sir, it was 6457 you inquired after, but,
of course, 6457 is dead. We agreed, after examining certain
discrepancies, that it was 6459 you were referring to.

Pause

ROOTE (*expressionless*)

Did we?

The lights fade on the office. They go up on the sitting room. MISS
CUTTS *and* LAMB *enter the sitting room.*

LAMB

That was fun, I must say. You know you really play extra-
ordinarily well, Miss Cutts.

CUTTS

Do I?

LAMB

Oh, excellent. I enjoyed it immensely.

MISS CUTTS *sits.* LAMB *goes to the coffee machine.*

LAMB

Black or white?

CUTTS

Black.

LAMB (*chuckling*)

I must say I got the surprise of my life, you know, when you
came up to me this morning and asked me if I played table
tennis. What I mean is, considering we've never spoken to
each other before.

He gives her a coffee.

It was really very nice of you.
Do you play often?

CUTTS

Not often.

LAMB

Well, it's a damn good piece of luck that our rotas coincide at
this time of the morning, isn't it? It'll be something to look
forward to, a game of ping-pong. I haven't played for ages.

Pause. He sits with his coffee.

Do you like it here?

CUTTS

Oh, I do. It's so rewarding.

LAMB

Your work?

CUTTS

Terribly rewarding.

LAMB

You've been here some time, of course?

CUTTS

Mmnn. Oh yes.

LAMB

What about Mr. Roote? How do you get on with him?

CUTTS

Oh, such a charming person. So genuine.

LAMB

Yes, I'm sure he is. I haven't really ... spoken to him yet.
Although I expect I will be meeting him, very soon now.

He stands, walks about.

I only wish I had a bit more to do. I'm a very energetic sort of chap, you know. Tremendous mental energy. I'm the sort of chap who's always *thinking* – you know what I mean? Then, when I've thought about something, I like to put it into action. I mean, I think a lot about the patients, you see.

Pause

You have quite a bit to do with them, I suppose?

CUTTS

Mmmn . . . . . .

LUSH *walks quickly into the sitting room.*

LUSH

Have you seen Gibbs?

LAMB

Gibbs?

LUSH *goes.*

What a curious thing. Did you hear that, Miss Cutts? That was Lush. He asked if we'd seen Gibbs.

MISS CUTTS *is leaning back in her chair.*

CUTTS

Mmnn?

LAMB

Lush. Popped his head in the door just now. Asked if we'd seen Gibbs.

CUTTS

And have we?

LAMB

I haven't.

Pause

You know, I ... I haven't really got used to this place.

Pause

Do you know what I mean? I wouldn't say this to anyone else but you, of course. The fact is, I haven't made much contact with any of the others. Hogg said good morning to me in a very nice way about a week ago when I bumped into him near the gym, but I haven't seen him since. (*With sudden briskness.*) No, you see, what happened was this – the Ministry said to me, I was working in one of their other departments at the time, doing something quite different – well, anyway, they called me up and they said to me – 'You've been posted'. Well, I'd heard about this place, of course. I was delighted. But ... but what exactly is the post, I said. You'll learn that when you get down there, they said, but we think you've got the right qualifications.

Pause

That's what they said. That was over a year ago.

Pause

And I've never learned who the man was I took over from, and I've never found out why he left, either. Anyway I'm pretty sure he wasn't doing the job I'm doing. Or if he was doing the same job he wasn't doing it in exactly the same way. The whole rota's been altered since he left, for a start. He couldn't have been doing my rota, and if he wasn't doing my rota he can hardly be said to have been doing my job. Rotas make all the difference.

Pause

I mean, my job, for instance. I have to see that all the gates are locked outside the building and that all the patients' doors are locked inside the building. It gives me exercise, I'll say that. It takes me two hours and six minutes, approximately, to try every gate and every door, then I can stand still for ten minutes, then off I go again. I have the regulation breaks, of course. Breakfast, lunch, tea and dinner. Still, I feel a bit whacked when my shift's over, I must admit. But as I said it gives me time to think — not when I'm testing the locks, of course — but in between locks — it gives me time to think, and mostly I think about the patients. I get some very good ideas while I think, honestly. As a matter of fact, I hear one receives a little token of esteem, sometimes — I mean after a certain period. I've got a feeling that mine's almost due.

Pause

Perhaps it might even be promotion.

Pause

Quite frankly, I can't make much more progress with this job I was allocated. There's not enough scope. I wish I could deal with the patients — directly. I've thought out a number of schemes, you know, ideas, for a really constructive, progressive approach to the patients — in fact, I've sent them in to the office. Haven't heard anything yet. I think possibly what's happening is that on the evidence of these schemes I sent in they're considering promotion. Look, I want to ask you, these schemes of mine — you know, the ones I've sent in to the office — do you think that was the right place to send them, or should I have handed them in personally to someone? The point is, who?

MISS CUTTS *looks at her watch. She stands.*

CUTTS

Will you excuse me? I'm afraid I have an appointment.

She goes to the door. LAMB *follows.*

LAMB

You're the only friend I've got here, to be quite frank. I don't seem to be able to ... reach the others. Don't know why. After all, I share their interests. Wouldn't you say?

They go out.

The lights fade on the sitting room. They go up on the office. ROOTE *and* GIBBS *are in the same positions.*

ROOTE *(deliberately)*

Well, how is 6459 getting on?

GIBBS

She's given birth to a boy, sir.

Pause

ROOTE

She ... has ... what?

GIBBS

Given birth, sir.

ROOTE

To ... a what?

GIBBS

A boy, sir.

Pause

ROOTE

I think you've gone too far, Gibbs.

GIBBS

Not me, sir, I assure you.

ROOTE *leans across the desk.*

ROOTE

Given birth?

GIBBS

Yes, sir.

ROOTE

To a child?

GIBBS

Yes, sir.

ROOTE

On these premises?

GIBBS

On the fourth floor, sir.

ROOTE *rises, leans over the desk to* GIBBS, *about to speak, unable to speak, turns, leaves the desk, walks heavily across the room.*

ROOTE

Sex?

GIBBS

Male.

ROOTE *sinks on to the sofa.*

ROOTE

This has made my morning. It really has made my morning.

He takes a pair of glasses out of his pocket, puts them on and looks across the room to GIBBS.

I'm dumbstruck. Quite thunderstruck. Absolutely thunderstruck! This has never happened before. Never! In all the years I've been here, in all the years my predecessor was here. And I'm quite certain never before him. To spend years and years, winter after winter, trying to perfect the working of an institution so fragile in its conception and execution, so fragile the boundary between the achievement of one's aspirations and their collapse, not only one's own aspirations; rather the aspirations of a whole community, a tradition, an ideal; such a delicately wrought concept of participation between him who is to be treated and him who is to treat that it defies analysis; trying to sustain this fine, fine balance, finer than a ... finer than a ...... far, far finer. Year after year, and so refined the operation that the softest breath, the breath of a ... feather ... can send the whole thing tottering into chaos, into ignominy, to the death and cancellation of all our hopes. Goodness gracious.

He stands.

As my predecessor said, on one unforgettable occasion: 'Order, gentlemen, for God's sake, order!' I remember the silence, row upon row of electrified faces, he with his golden forelock, his briar burning, upright and commanding, a soldier's stance, looking down from the platform. The gymnasium was packed to suffocation, standing room only. The lucky ones were perched on vaulting horses, hanging without movement from the wallbars. 'Order, gentlemen,' he said, 'for the love of Mike!' As one man we looked out of the window at Mike, and gazed at the statue – covered in snow, it so happened, then as now. Mike! The predecessor of my predecessor, the predecessor of us all, the man who laid the foundation stone, the man who introduced the first patient, the man who, after the incredible hordes of patients, or would-be patients, had followed him through town and country, hills and valleys, waited under hedges, lined the bridges and sat six feet deep in the ditch, opened institution after institution up and down the country, rest homes, nursing homes, convalescent homes, sanatoria. He was sanctioned by the Ministry, revered by the populace, subsidised by the State. He had set in motion an activity for humanity, of humanity and by humanity. And the keyword was order.

He turns to GIBBS.

I, Gibbs, have tried to preserve that order. A vocation, in fact. And you choose Christmas morning to come and tell me this. I tell you quite frankly I smell disaster.

GIBBS

With respect, sir, I can't see that the matter is of such extreme significance.

ROOTE

You can't? Have we ever, to your knowledge, given birth to a child on these premises before?

GIBBS

Not to my knowledge, sir.

ROOTE

Therefore we have no yardstick. As a mathematician you will appreciate that we have nothing to measure this event by so that we can with ease assess its implications.

GIBBS

I am not a mathematician, sir.

ROOTE

Well, you look like one!

He pockets his glasses, sits at the desk.

Right! There's work to be done. Find the culprit. Who is he?

GIBBS

That, sir, we have not yet been able to ascertain.

ROOTE

Why not? Have you asked the patient?

GIBBS

Yes, sir.

ROOTE

What did she say?

GIBBS

She was ... noncommital, sir. She said she couldn't be
entirely sure since most of the staff have had relations with
her in this last year.

ROOTE

Most of the staff?

GIBBS

According to her statement, sir.

ROOTE *rubs his mouth.*

ROOTE

Which one *is* 6459?

GIBBS

She's a woman in her thirties –

ROOTE

That means nothing to me, get on with it, what does she look
like? Perhaps I know her.

GIBBS

Oh, there's no doubt that you know her, sir.

ROOTE

What does she look like?

Pause

GIBBS

Fattish.

ROOTE

Darkheaded?

GIBBS (*sitting*)

Not fairheaded, sir.

Pause

ROOTE

Small?

GIBBS

Certainly not tall.

Pause

ROOTE

Quite a sensual sort of face?

GIBBS

Quite sensual, yes, sir.

ROOTE

Yes.

Pause

Yes, she's got a sensual sort of face, hasn't she?

GIBBS

I should say it was sensual, sir, yes.

ROOTE

Wobbles when she walks?

GIBBS

Oh, possibly a trifle, sir.

ROOTE

Yes, she wobbles. She wobbles in her left buttock.

GIBBS

Her left, sir?

ROOTE

Well, one of them. I'm sure of it.

GIBBS

Yes, she has a slight wobble, sir.

ROOTE

Yes, of course she has.

Pause

She's got a slight wobble. Whenever she walks anywhere . . .
she wobbles. Likes eating toffees, too . . . when she can get
any.

GIBBS

Quite true, sir.

Pause

ROOTE

No – I don't think I know her.

Pause

And you say a number of the staff have had relations with this woman, do you?

GIBBS

Apparently, sir.

ROOTE (*standing*)

Well, one of them's slipped up, hasn't he? One of them's not been using his head! His know-how! Common or garden horsesense! I don't mind the men dipping their wicks on occasion. It can't be avoided. It's got to go somewhere. Besides that, it's in the interests of science. If a member of the staff decides that for the good of a female patient some degree of copulation is necessary then two birds are killed with one stone! It does no harm to either party. At least, that's how I've found it in my experience. (*With emphasis.*) But we all know the rule! Never ride barebacked. Always take precautions. Otherwise complications set in. Never ride barebacked and always send in a report. After all, the reactions of the patient have to be tabulated, compared with others, filed, stamped and if possible verified! It stands to reason. (*Grimly.*) Well, I can tell you something, Gibbs, one thing is blatantly clear to me. *Someone* hasn't been sending in his report!

GIBBS

Quite, sir.

ROOTE

Who?

GIBBS *sits on the sofa and puts his hand to his mouth.*

GIBBS

I think I know the man.

ROOTE

Who?

GIBBS (*thoughtfully*)

Yes, it's suddenly come to me. How absurd I didn't realise it before.

ROOTE

Who, for God's sake?

GIBBS

I'd prefer to have the matter verified, sir, before I . . . bring him before you.

ROOTE

All right. But find him. The good name of this establishment depends on it.

ROOTE *sits at the desk.* GIBBS *goes to the door.*

GIBBS

What shall I do about the baby, sir?

ROOTE

Get rid of it.

GIBBS

The mother would have to go with it, sir.

ROOTE

Why?

GIBBS

Can't live without the mother.

ROOTE

Why not?

GIBBS

The mother feeds it.

ROOTE

I know that! Do you think I'm an idiot? My mother fed me, didn't she?

GIBBS

Mine fed me.

ROOTE

But mine fed me!

Pause

I remember.

Pause

Isn't there a wet nurse in the house? If there's a wet nurse in the house the baby can go with the wet nurse and the mother can stay here.

GIBBS

There's no wet nurse among the staff, sir.

ROOTE

I should hope not. I'm thinking about the understaff, the kitchen staff, the cleaning staff. Find out if there's a wet nurse among the understaff and get the thing in motion.

GIBBS

Don't you think the mother might miss the baby, sir?

ROOTE

I won't miss it. Will you miss it?

GIBBS

No, sir. I won't miss it.

ROOTE

Then why should the mother miss it?

They stare at each other. There is a knock on the door.

ROOTE

Who is it?

CUTTS

Me.

ROOTE

Gibbs, find that father. Come in!

Enter MISS CUTTS.

CUTTS (*to* GIBBS)

Hullo.

GIBBS

I'll keep you in touch with developments, sir.

ROOTE

That's very thoughtful of you.

GIBBS *goes out.* MISS CUTTS *sits on the sofa.* ROOTE *rises, goes to the sofa and sits next to her.*

ROOTE

I'm exhausted.

CUTTS

You know, I think that man's frightened of me.

ROOTE

Rubbish.

CUTTS

He never speaks to me. He never says a single word to me.
And not only that, he never ... he never looks at me. I can
only think I must frighten him in some way.

ROOTE

What do you mean, never speaks to you? He's obliged to
speak to you. You're working together, aren't you?

CUTTS

Oh yes, he talks shop to me. We discuss the patients, naturally. We were discussing one of the patients ... only yesterday. But he never speaks to me socially.

ROOTE

Which patient?

CUTTS

Or do you think he's taken with me? Do you think that he just
finds me too attractive to look at?

ROOTE

Which patient were you discussing?

CUTTS

But I can't say I like him. He's so cold. Oh, I like men to be cold — but not as cold as that. Oh, no, he's much too cold. You know, I think I'll ask him. I think I'll ask him whether he's taken with me or whether I frighten him. I mean, one might as well know.

ROOTE

Do you know what I've just heard? One of the patients has just had a baby.

CUTTS

A baby? But how?

ROOTE

As large as life. And under my auspices. It's nothing short of criminal.

CUTTS

But how did she manage it?

ROOTE

She had an accomplice.

CUTTS

No? Who?

ROOTE

That's what we've got to find out.

CUTTS

But which patient? Who is she?

ROOTE

I don't know her.

MISS CUTTS *leans back.*

CUTTS (*dreamily*)

I bet she feels very feminine now.

ROOTE (*vacantly, staring into space*)

She's always been feminine.

CUTTS

Do you think I'm feminine enough, darling? Or do you think
I should be more feminine?

ROOTE *is still abstracted.*

Darling. You don't think I'm too masculine, do you? I mean,
you don't think I could go even further? Do you?

ROOTE (*absently, muttering*)

Yes, yes why not?

CUTTS

You *do* think I should be more feminine?

ROOTE

What?

CUTTS

But you always say I'm feminine enough!

ROOTE

You are feminine enough.

CUTTS

Then if I'm feminine enough why do you want me to be more feminine?

ROOTE

I don't, I don't.

CUTTS

But you just said you did!

ROOTE

I don't, I don't!

CUTTS (*at a great pace*)

Because it would be awful if you really thought that I was letting you down in the most important aspect of the relationship between any man and any woman –

ROOTE

You're quite feminine enough!!

Pause

CUTTS

You really mean it?

ROOTE

Yes. (*He runs his hand through his hair.*) I've had the most wearing morning. On top of everything else one of the patients has died.

CUTTS

Died?

ROOTE

Dead.

CUTTS

Oh my poor sweet, and I've been nasty to you.

She kisses him.

Let me massage you. Come into the bedroom. Let me do your neck.

ROOTE

Yes. Do my neck.

They go into the bedroom.
The lights go down on the office. They go up on the sitting room.

GIBBS *enters. He sits at the low table, takes out a pack of cards and begins to play patience, very deliberately.*
LUSH *appears at the head of the stairway and descends.*
Suddenly a long sigh is heard, amplified.
LUSH *stops.* GIBBS, *about to place a card, stops. A long keen is heard, amplified.*
LUSH *looks up.* GIBBS, *card in hand, looks up.*
A laugh is heard, amplified, dying away.
Silence.
LUSH *descends the steps, enters the room.*

LUSH

Hullo, Charlie.

He closes the door and comes to the table. GIBBS, *after a glance at him, places another card.* LUSH, *inspects the state of the game.* GIBBS *scatters the cards.*

How's tricks, Charlie? (*Pause.*) What you been doing with yourself? (*Pause.*) Mmnn? (*Pause.*) Having a nice Christmas?

GIBBS

What do you want?

LUSH

What do you think of the weather?

GIBBS *collects the cards and puts them into a card case.*

GIBBS

You want something. What is it?

LUSH

I don't want anything, Gibbs. I've got something to report, that's all.

GIBBS

What is it?

LUSH

Don't get tense, Gibbs. After all, we're all buddies, aren't we? We're all in the game together.

GIBBS

You want to report something. What is it?

LUSH

Actually I want to ask you something first.

GIBBS

What?

LUSH

How's 6459 getting on?

Pause

GIBBS

You want to report something. What is it?

LUSH

I hear she's given birth.

GIBBS

It's none of your business.

LUSH

Oh, we're all concerned, you know. We're all concerned.

GIBBS

Listen, Lush. I'm not prepared to have any kind of conversation with you whatsoever. If you've got something to report report it and don't make a fool of yourself.

LUSH

Are you the father, Gibbs?

GIBBS *sits back and folds his arms.*

LUSH

Or the old man. Is the old man the father?

LUSH *sits*.

Who's going to carry the can? Miss Cutts? Do you think she's
the father? We're all terribly excited, you know. Can't think
what to call it. The kid's got to have a name, after all. What do
you think yourself? I think something that'll remind him of
this establishment when he grows up, don't you? His birth
place. Of course, it depends on the father's name, doesn't it?
I mean, the father might like the boy to be named after him.
You know, if the father's name was John then the boy would
be named John too. Do you see what I mean? The same name
as the father.

GIBBS
You know, Lush, I don't know how you've lasted here.
You're incompetent, you're unwholesome and you're offen-
sive. You're the most totally bloody useless bugger I've ever
come across.

LUSH
I can see you're in one of your moods today, Gibbs, so I
suppose I'd better report to you what I came to report to you.

GIBBS
What is it?

LUSH
The mother of 6457 came to see me today.

GIBBS
The mother of 6457?

LUSH
Yes, you know. The one who died. He died last Thursday.
From heart failure.

GIBBS

His mother?

LUSH

Yes.

GIBBS

How did she get in?

LUSH

That's what baffled me. It did. It quite baffled me. How on earth did she get in? I wondered. How did she do it? Why wasn't she stopped? Why did no-one demand her credentials? It baffled me. Then – in a flash! – the answer came. She'd been hiding all night in the shrubbery, waiting for Tubb to leave his cubby-hole and take a leak, which eventually he did, and then she just darted in, like a shot off a shovel. Simple. We really tend to overlook the simple cunning of the simple. Would you like her description?

GIBBS

No. What did she want?

LUSH

She wanted to know how her son was getting on. She said that when her son came here she was told he needed peace and expert attention and that she would be hearing from us in due course, and that in fact it was now a year since she had seen him and she wanted to know how he was getting on.

GIBBS

What did you say?

LUSH

I said – A year? You haven't seen him for a year? But that's ridiculous. Didn't you come down for Mother's Day, or Thanksgiving Day, or for the annual summer picnic for patients, staff, relatives and friends? Weren't you invited to the Halloween Feast, the May Dance, the October Revival, the Old Boys and Girls supper and social? Dancing on the lawn, cold buffets on the flat roof, midnight croquet, barbecued boar by the lake? None of this? I never knew about it, she said. What! I said. The autumn art exhibition, the monthly concert of orchestral music in the bandroom, the half-yearly debate on a selected topic, held traditionally in the men's changing room? The pageant? The unveiling? The Festival of One-Act Plays, judged by Miss Daisy Cutts, L.R.M.B., A.C.A., our dramatic instructor? You came down, I said, for none of these activities and ceremonies through which we from time immemorial engage and channel our patients' energies? Oh dear, she said, I was never told. Obviously a clerical error, I said, I shall have it looked into. But, I said, it is a shame that you haven't seen him, since he is now departed from us.

GIBBS

What!

LUSH

He was moved some time ago, I said, to a convalescent home. But I thought this was a convalescent home, said 6457's mother. (*He laughs.*) Silly woman. A convalescent home? I countered, no, no, no, not at all, not at all, whatever gave you that idea? This is a rest home. Oh, said 6457's mother. I see. Well, wasn't he getting enough rest here that they had to send him to a convalescent home? Ah, Mrs 6457, I said, it's not quite so simple as that. It's not *quite* so *simple* as *that*. In a rest home, you see, you do not merely rest. Nor, in a convalescent home, do you merely convalesce. No, no, in both institutions, you see, you are obliged to work and play and join in daily communal activity to the greatest possible extent. Otherwise the concepts of rest and convalescence are rendered meaningless. Don't for a moment either imagine that the terms rest and convalescence are synonymous. No, no, no, no. They represent, you see, stages. Sometimes one must rest first and then convalesce. Sometimes the reverse. Either course, of course, is only decided after the best interests of the patient have been taken into account. So, I continued, you can rest assured that if your son was moved from here to another place it was in his best interests, and only after the most extensive research into his case, the wealth and weight of all the expert opinion in this establishment, where some of the leading brains in this country are concentrated; after a world of time, care, gathering and accumulating of mass upon mass upon mass of relevant evidence, document, affidavit, tape recordings, played both backwards and forwards, deep into the depth of the night; hours of time, attention to the most minute detail, unstinting labour, unflagging effort, scrupulous attachment to the matter in hand and meticulous examination of all aspects of the question had determined the surest and most beneficial course your son's case might take. The conclusion, after this supreme example of applied dedication, was to send your son to a convalescent home, where we are sure he will be content.

Pause

I also pointed out that we had carte blanche from the Ministry. She left much moved by my recital.

Pause

GIBBS
Thank you for your report, Mr. Lush.

LUSH

No congratulations?

GIBBS *consults his watch and goes to the internal telephone.*

GIBBS

Will you excuse me?

LUSH

I'll excuse you for the time being, Gibbs.

He goes out.

GIBBS (*into the phone*)

22, please. (*Pause.*) Sir? Gibbs here. I'd like to speak with Miss Cutts, if I may, with reference to that matter we were discussing earlier. Thank you. (*Pause.*) Miss Cutts? I believe you know a man called Lamb. He's on the staff. Yes. I would be obliged if you would collect him and bring him to number one interviewing room. When I join you, perhaps you would be so kind as to go to 1A control room. I shall be glad of your participation. Thank you.

He replaces the receiver, and leaves the room.
The lights fade on the sitting room.
The lights go up on the left stage area, including the stairway.
MISS CUTTS, *followed by* LAMB, *appears at the foot of the stairway. They ascend.* MISS CUTTS *is wearing a white coat.*

LAMB

But what do you think it's all about? I mean, he wanted to see me particularly, did he?

CUTTS

Oh yes. Particularly.

LAMB (*stopping*)

But he didn't say why?

CUTTS

No.

LAMB

You know, I don't know why, but as soon as you said 'Mr Gibbs wants to see you,' I felt an extraordinary *uplift*. Isn't it amazing? Really, I felt uplifted. I still do, I must say . . .

They go out of sight. The lights come up on the sound-proof room. MISS CUTTS *and* LAMB *enter the sound-proof room.*

It's very curious, I know, but I really feel it's . . . significant. I mean, why should I suddenly feel uplifted . . . You know, I can't help thinking, I know it's very silly of me, but I can't help thinking this is something to do with my promotion. Do you think he's read my schemes? I mean, why else would he send for me when I was on duty?

GIBBS *enters the room from another door. He wears a white coat.*

CUTTS

Mr Gibbs, have you met Mr Lamb?

GIBBS

How do you do?

LAMB

How do you do?

CUTTS

Would you excuse me a minute, please?

She leaves the room by the other door.

GIBBS

Would you take a seat, Mr Lamb?

LAMB

This one?

GIBBS

Yes, this one.

LAMB *sits.*

GIBBS

I'm delighted to meet you.

LAMB

Thank you. I must say I've always enjoyed my work here tremendously . . . I mean, you really get the feeling here that something . . . *important* is going on, something really valuable, and to be associated with it in any way can't be seen in any other light than as a privilege.

GIBBS

That's a very heartening attitude.

LAMB

Oh, I really mean it, quite sincerely.

GIBBS

Good. I've heard a great deal about you, you know.

LAMB

Really?

GIBBS

Yes, there's quite a lot I'd like to talk to you about, when we have the time. But in the meanwhile I wonder ... if you'd give me a helping hand?

LAMB

I'd be quite delighted!

GIBBS

That's the spirit! (*With no undue emphasis.*) Miss Cutts, could you come down, please?

LAMB

What did you say?

GIBBS

I beg your pardon?

LAMB

Did you speak to Miss Cutts just now?

GIBBS

Yes, I asked her to come down.

LAMB

But where from?

GIBBS

From room 1A.

LAMB

But did she hear you?

GIBBS

Oh yes.

LAMB

How?

GIBBS (*pointing*)

That mike. It's just been switched on.

LAMB (*laughing*)

Oh, I see.

Pause

Curious kind of room, isn't it?

GIBBS

It's a sound-proof room.

Enter MISS CUTTS.

Ah, Miss Cutts. Now, Lamb, what I'd like is for you to help us with some little tests. Will you do that?

LAMB

Tests? I'd be delighted. That's what I hoped I'd be doing when I first came down here.

GIBBS

Really? Good.

LAMB

What kind of tests are they?

GIBBS

Experiments.

LAMB

Oh, I see.

GIBBS

Well, we have a very willing subject, Miss Cutts.

CUTTS

We do.

GIBBS

Oh by the way, Lamb, Merry Christmas.

LAMB

Thanks. Merry Christmas to you. And to you, Miss Cutts.

CUTTS

Thank you. And to you. (*To* GIBBS.) And to you too.

GIBBS

And to you. (*Briskly.*) Now — perhaps you would fit the electrodes to Mr. Lamb's wrists.

LAMB

Electrodes?

GIBBS

Yes.

CUTTS

Could I have your hand, Mr. Lamb?

MISS CUTTS *brings an electrode from her pocket and attaches it to* LAMB's *wrist.*

CUTTS

Now the other one.

She attaches a second electrode.

LAMB

What are they . . . exactly?

GIBBS

They're electric. You don't feel anything, of course. Best thing to do is forget all about them.

CUTTS

Now I'm going to plug in.

She bends at the wall, where, through a hole, three leads protrude. She picks up two and returns to LAMB.

GIBBS

Now she's going to plug in. You see the little socket on each of those electrodes? They're for the plug. (*He watches* MISS CUTTS *plug in.*) That's right. First plug in A, then plug in B. Right. Now you're plugged in.

LAMB

Oh, you've ... got to be plugged in, have you?

GIBBS (*with a chuckle*)

Oh yes, got to be plugged in. The leads go right through the wall and up to the control room, you see. We're plugged in the other end.

LAMB

You?

GIBBS (*laughing*)

No, no, not me. You. Into the receiving set.

LAMB

Oh, I see. What are these ... what are these electrodes for, exactly?

GIBBS

They measure electrical potential on the skin.

LAMB

Oh.

GIBBS

Engendered by neural activity, of course.

LAMB

Oh, of course.

GIBBS

Electrical impulses, in a word. You can imagine how

important they are and yet how little we know about them. Right. Now the earphones.

MISS CUTTS *stoops, picks up the earphones, attaches them to* LAMB's *head.*

LAMB

Earphones?

GIBBS

Yes, same principle. Plugged in at the socket on your head, plugged in at the other end in our control room. (*Cheeringly*.) Don't worry, they're nice long leads, all of them. Plenty of leeway. No danger of strangulation.

LAMB (*laughing*)

Oh yes. Good.

GIBBS

By the way, your predecessor used to give us a helping hand occasionally, too, you know. Before you came, of course.

LAMB

My predecessor?

CUTTS

Could you just keep still a second, Mr Lamb, while I plug in the earphones?

LAMB *is still. She plugs.*

Thank you.

GIBBS

Comfortable?

LAMB

Yes, thank you. My predecessor, did you say?

GIBBS

Yes, the chap you took over from.

LAMB

Oh! Did he really? Oh, good. I've often wondered what he
... did, exactly. Oh good, I'm ... glad I'm following in a
tradition.

They all chuckle.

Have you any idea where he is now?

GIBBS

No, I don't think I do know where he is now. Do you know
where he is, Miss Cutts?

CUTTS

No, I'm afraid I don't.

GIBBS

No, I'm afraid we don't really know. He's not here, anyway.
That's certain. Now what I want you to do is to sit perfectly
still. Relax completely. Don't think about a thing. That's
right. Now you see that light up there. Ignore it. It might
go on and off at regular or irregular intervals. Take no notice.
Sit perfectly still. Quite comfortable?

LAMB

Yes, thanks.

GIBBS

Jolly good. Don't go to sleep, will you? We're awfully grate-
ful to you, old chap, for helping us.

LAMB

It's a pleasure.

GIBBS *places his hand briefly on* LAMB's *shoulder.*
MISS CUTTS *and* GIBBS *go out.*
LAMB *sits. Silence. He shifts, concentrates. The light, which is red, flicks on and off.*
Silence. Suddenly LAMB *jolts rigid, his hands go to his earphones, he is propelled from the chair, falls to his knees, twisting from side to side, still clutching his earphones, emitting high-pitched cries.*

He suddenly stops still.

The red light is still flickering.
He looks up. He sits in the chair, emits a short chuckle.
The red light stops.

The voice of MISS CUTTS *is heard.*

CUTTS

Would you say you were an excitable person?

LAMB *looks up.*

LAMB

Not . . . not unduly, no.

The voice of GIBBS *is heard.*

GIBBS

Would you say you were a moody person?

LAMB

Moody? No, I wouldn't say I was moody – well, sometimes occasionally I –

CUTTS

Do you ever get fits of depression?

LAMB

Well, I wouldn't call them depression, exactly –

GIBBS

Would you say you were a sociable person?

LAMB

Well, that's not a very easy question to answer, really. I try, I certainly try to be sociable, I mean I think it should be the aim of any one interested in human nature to try to mix, to better his understanding of it. I –

CUTTS

Do you find yourself unaccountably happy one moment and unaccountably unhappy the next?

LAMB

It's strange you should say that because –

GIBBS

Do you often do things which you regret in the morning?

LAMB

Regret? Things I regret? Well, it depends what you mean by often, really. I mean, when you say often –

CUTTS

Are you often puzzled by women?

LAMB

Women?

GIBBS

Men.

LAMB

Men? Well, I was just going to answer the question about women –

GIBBS

Do you often feel puzzled?

LAMB

Puzzled?

GIBBS

By women.

LAMB

Women?

CUTTS

Men.

LAMB

Uh – now just a minute, I . . . do you want separate answers or a joint answer?

CUTTS

After your day's work, do you ever feel tired, edgy?

GIBBS

Fretty?

CUTTS

Irritable?

GIBBS

At a loose end?

CUTTS

Morose?

GIBBS

Frustrated?

CUTTS

Morbid?

GIBBS

Unable to concentrate?

CUTTS

Unable to sleep?

GIBBS

Unable to eat?

CUTTS

Unable to remain seated?

GIBBS

Unable to stand upright?

CUTTS

Lustful?

GIBBS

Indolent?

CUTTS

On heat?

GIBBS

Randy?

CUTTS

Full of desire?

GIBBS

Full of energy?

CUTTS

Full of dread?

GIBBS

Drained?

CUTTS

Of energy?

GIBBS

Of dread?

CUTTS

Of desire?

Pause

LAMB

Well, it's difficult to say, really —

LAMB *jolts rigid, his hands go to his earphones, he is propelled from the chair, falls to his knees, twisting from side to side, still*

clutching his earphones, emitting highpitched cries.
The red light flicks on and off.

He suddenly stops still.

The red light is still flickering.
He looks up. He sits in the chair, emits a short chuckle.
The red light stops.

CUTTS

Are you virgo intacta?

LAMB

What?

CUTTS

Are you virgo intacta?

LAMB

Oh, I say, that's rather embarrassing. I mean, in front of a lady—

CUTTS

Are you virgo intacta?

LAMB

Yes, I am, actually. I'll make no secret of it.

CUTTS

Have you always been virgo intacta?

LAMB

Oh yes, always. Always.

CUTTS

From the word go?

LAMB

Go? Oh yes. From the word go.

GIBBS

What is the law of the Wolf Cub Pack?

LAMB

The cub gives in to the Old Wolf, the cub does not give in to himself.

GIBBS

When you were a boy scout were you most proficient at somersault, knots, leap frog, hopping, skipping, balancing, cleanliness, recitation or ball games?

LAMB

Well, actually, I never became a boy scout proper. I was a wolf cub, of course, but I never became a boy scout. I don't know why, actually. I've forgotten . . . to be frank. But I was a cub.

CUTTS

Do women frighten you?

GIBBS

Their clothes?

CUTTS

Their shoes?

GIBBS

Their voices?

CUTTS

Their laughter?

GIBBS

Their stares?

CUTTS

Their way of walking?

GIBBS

Their way of sitting?

CUTTS

Their way of smiling?

GIBBS

Their way of talking?

CUTTS

Their mouths?

GIBBS

Their hands?

CUTTS

Their legs?

GIBBS

Their teeth?

CUTTS

Their shins?

GIBBS

Their cheeks?

CUTTS

Their ears?

GIBBS

Their calves?

CUTTS

Their arms?

GIBBS

Their toes?

CUTTS

Their eyes?

GIBBS

Their knees?

CUTTS

Their thighs?

Pause

LAMB

Well, it depends what you mean by frighten –

GIBBS

Do you ever wake up in the middle of the night?

LAMB

Sometimes, yes, for a glass of water.

GIBBS

Do you ever feel you would like to join a group of people in which group common assumptions are shared and common principles observed?

LAMB

Well, I am a member of such a group, here, in this establishment.

GIBBS

Which establishment?

LAMB

This one.

GIBBS

Which establishment?

LAMB

This one.

GIBBS

You are a member of this establishment?

LAMB

Of course.

Silence

(*Looking up*.) Mmnn?

Any more questions?

I'm quite ready for another question.

I'm quite ready.

I'm rather enjoying this, you know.

Oh, by the way, what was that extraordinary sound?

It gave me quite a start, I must admit.

Are you all right up there?

You haven't finished your questions, have you?

I'm ready whenever you are.

Silence

LAMB *sits.*
The red light begins to flick on and off.
LAMB *looks up, stares at it.*
We hear the loud click of a switch from the control room.
The microphone in the room has been switched off.
*The red light gradually grows in strength, until it consumes
the room.*
LAMB *sits still.*

Curtain

Act Two

ROOTE's *office. Night.*
ROOTE *is at his desk, examining some papers.*
LUSH *is at the window, looking out.*

ROOTE (*without looking up*)
What are you looking at, Lush?

LUSH
The yard, sir.

ROOTE
Anyone about?

LUSH
Not a soul.

ROOTE
What's the weather like?

LUSH
The snow has turned to slush.

ROOTE
Ah.

Pause

Has the wind got up?

LUSH
No. No wind at all.

ROOTE *turns a page*.

ROOTE (*muttering*)

No wind, eh? (*He examines the page, then slams it onto the desk*.) I can't read a word of this! It's indecipherable. What's the matter with this man Hogg? Why can't he type his reports out like everyone else? I can't read this writing. It's unreadable.

LUSH

His typewriter's out of action, sir.

ROOTE

What's the matter with it?

LUSH

It seems to have got stuck, sir.

ROOTE

Stuck?

LUSH

It just won't move at all.

ROOTE

Well, there must be an obstacle somewhere, or something.

LUSH

It looked like rust to me.

ROOTE

Rust? What are you talking about? It's a brand new typewriter. It's a Ministry typewriter. We had a whole cartload sent down from the Ministry – when was it? – a couple of months ago. Brand new. I've still got the invoice somewhere. Rust. Never heard such rubbish. Anyway, I can't sit here all night trying to work this out. (*He puts the papers in a drawer, goes to the drinks cabinet, takes out a bottle of whisky and pours himself a drink.*) I've had enough this week. I never leave this desk, do you know that? Sun up to sundown. Day in day out. It's the price you have to pay for being in command, for being responsible for the whole shoot. As I am. The whole damn shoot. (*He drinks.*)

LUSH *walks to the cabinet, collects a glass and pours himself a drink.*

ROOTE
When?

LUSH

You do leave this desk quite often, though, don't you, sir?

ROOTE

What?

LUSH

I say, in point of fact, you do leave this desk quite often, don't you?

ROOTE

When?

LUSH

When you go and visit the patients, for instance.

ROOTE

That's purely in the line of duty. It's not relaxation. I meant relaxation. I wasn't talking about the line of duty.

LUSH

Oh.

ROOTE

Anyway, I've given up visiting the patients. It's not worth it.
A waste of energy.

LUSH

What an extraordinary thing to say, Mr Roote.

ROOTE

Don't Mr Roote me.

LUSH

But I never expected to hear you say a thing like that, Mr
Roote.

ROOTE

I said don't Mr Roote me!

LUSH

But I always understood that you looked upon visits to the
patients from the head of this establishment as one of the
most important features in the running of this establishment
... Mr. Roote.

ROOTE

Listen! I give you leeway. But don't think I give you that
much leeway.

LUSH

No, sir.

ROOTE

Don't think I can't squash you on a plate as easy as look at
you.

LUSH

Yes, sir.

ROOTE

As easy as look at you, Lush.

LUSH

Quite, sir.

ROOTE

So don't give me any more lip, you understand me? Otherwise you're liable to find yourself in trouble.

LUSH

You know I harbour no illusions about my position, Colonel.

ROOTE

Don't call me Colonel!

LUSH

But you were a Colonel once, weren't you, Colonel?

ROOTE

I was. And a bloody good one too.

LUSH

If I may say so, you still possess considerable military bearing.

ROOTE

Really?

LUSH

Oh yes.

ROOTE

Well, it's not surprising.

LUSH

And the ability to be always one thought ahead of the next man.

ROOTE

It's a military characteristic.

LUSH

Really?

ROOTE

Oh yes. Of course, some of them aren't very bright, I must admit.

LUSH

Who?

ROOTE

Military men.

LUSH

Really? I'm sorry to hear that.

ROOTE

Yes, some of them tend to let the side down. They've got no foresight, that's what it is. They can't think clearly. They've got no vision. Vision's very important.

LUSH

You must have been quite a unique kind of man, sir, in your regiment.

ROOTE

Yes, well I . . . What do you mean?

LUSH

The age of the specialist is dead.

ROOTE

What?

LUSH

The age of the specialist is dead.

ROOTE

Oh. Dead. Yes.

LUSH

That's why I say you must have been quite a unique kind of
man, sir, in your regiment, being such an all-round man.

ROOTE

Yes, yes, there's something in that.

He perches on the desk.

LUSH

I mean, not only are you a scientist, but you have literary
ability, musical ability, knowledge of most schools of philos-
ophy, philology, photography, anthropology, cosmology,
theology, phytology, phytonomy, phytotomy –

ROOTE

Oh, no, no, not phytotomy.

LUSH

Not phytotomy?

ROOTE

I was always meaning to get round to phytotomy, of course, but . . . well, I've had so many other things to think about.

LUSH

Naturally.

ROOTE

But anyway, once you know something about phytonomy you're halfway there.

LUSH

Halfway where, sir?

ROOTE

To phytotomy!

Pause

Give us a drink.

LUSH *fills the glasses.*

LUSH

Why have you given up visiting the patients?

ROOTE

I've given up, that's all.

LUSH

But I thought you were getting results?

ROOTE (*staring at him*)

Cheers.

LUSH

Weren't you getting results?

ROOTE (*staring at him*)

Drink your whisky.

LUSH

But surely you achieved results with one patient very recently. What was the number? 6459, I think.

ROOTE *throws his whisky in* LUSH's *face.* LUSH *wipes his face.*

LUSH

Let me fill you up. (*He takes* ROOTE's *glass, pours, brings the glass to* ROOTE, *gives it to him.*) Yes, quite a substantial result, I should have thought.

ROOTE *throws his whisky in* LUSH's *face.* LUSH *wipes his face.* LUSH *takes* ROOTE's *glass, pours, brings the glass to* ROOTE, *gives it to him.*

But perhaps I'm thinking of 6457.

LUSH *grabs* ROOTE's *glass and holds it above his head, with his own. Slowly he lowers his own.*

Cheers.

He drinks, and then gives ROOTE *his glass.*

> ROOTE (*taking the glass, in a low voice*)
You're neglecting to call me sir, Lush. You're supposed to call me sir when you address me.

Pause

ROOTE *suddenly takes off his jacket, hangs it on the back of his chair and sits.*

God, the heat of this place. It's damn hot, isn't it? It's like a crematorium in here. Why is it suddenly so hot?

> LUSH
The snow has turned to slush, sir.

> ROOTE
Has it?

> LUSH
Very dangerous.

> ROOTE
It's a heatwave, that's what it is. (*A knock on the door*.) Who is it?

Enter GIBBS.

Oh no, what is it? Business at this hour? You sit down to have a quiet drink and what happens?

GIBBS

I have something to report, sir.

ROOTE

What? (GIBBS *looks at* LUSH.) Oh, never mind about him! What is it?

GIBBS

I don't approve of divulging official secrets to all and sundry, sir.

ROOTE

I know you don't approve! I don't approve! Nobody approves! But you've no alternative, have you?

GIBBS

Mr Lush could leave the room, sir.

ROOTE

Good God, what an impertinence! The man's my guest, do you understand that? Which is more than you bloodywell are! I've never heard of such a thing in all my life. He barges in here and tells me to chuck my own guest out of the room. Who do you think you are?

Pause

(*To* LUSH.) He gets on my wick sometimes – doesn't he you?

GIBBS

I ... apologise, sir, if I have been presumptuous.

ROOTE

Well, what's your business?

GIBBS

The father has been found.

ROOTE

No?

GIBBS

Found.

ROOTE (*rising*)

Found? So soon? In so short a space of time? Jiminy Cricket, that's quick work, Gibbs! (*He stands, shakes hands with* GIBBS.) Absolutely first class! (*He moves to* LUSH.) What do you think of that, eh, for a bit of quick work?

LUSH

Remarkable.

ROOTE

You see the way I train my staff? Alacrity! First and foremost, alacrity! Get on with it, don't muck about, don't dither, pick your man and pin him to the wall. Let your nose do your thinking for you and you won't go far wrong. That's what we try to do here, cultivate the habit of split second decisions. Right? Right, Gibbs?

GIBBS

Quite, sir.

ROOTE

Right, Lush?

LUSH

Quite, sir.

ROOTE

And it never fails. I'm pleased with you, Gibbs. Who is he?

GIBBS

A man called Lamb, sir.

ROOTE

Never heard of him.

ROOTE *sits, pours a drink and drinks*.

LUSH

Lamb? Surely not Lorna Lamb? Lorna Lamb in the dispensary department?

ROOTE

A man, not a woman, you bloody fool!

LUSH

Oh, I'm so sorry, I didn't quite ... What exactly has this person done?

Pause

ROOTE

Tell him what this person has done, Mr Gibbs.

GIBBS

A child has been born to one of the patients. It was considered a matter of the first importance to locate the father. This has now been done.

ROOTE

Lamb? Who the hell's Lamb? Do I know him?

GIBBS

I think it doubtful that you've ever met him, sir.

ROOTE

I don't even know what he looks like. A rapist on my own staff and I don't know what he looks like!

LUSH

Was it rape?

ROOTE

Of course it was rape. You don't think that sort of thing happens by consent, do you?

GIBBS

He's not a very important member of your staff, sir.

ROOTE

Well, if he's not important how did he get into the patient's room? You know as well as I do that only a very select handful of the personnel are allowed in the patients' rooms. How did he get in?

GIBBS

He tests the locks, sir, of all the rooms in the building. Either this particular lock was ... not locked, or he forced it.

ROOTE

It's unbelievable, isn't it, Lush, the things that go on?

LUSH

It almost is, sir.

ROOTE

The sabotage that goes on, under your very nose. Open the window. I'm suffocating. (LUSH *opens the window*.) Is that radiator hot?

LUSH *bends to the radiator and touches it.*

LUSH
Scalding, sir.

ROOTE
That's why I'm so hot.

LUSH
The night is warm, Mr Roote. The snow has turned to slush.

ROOTE
That's about the fifth time you've said the snow has turned to
slush!

GIBBS
It's quite true, sir. I noticed it myself.

ROOTE
I don't care whether it's true or not. I don't like to have a
thing repeated and repeated and repeated! Anyone would
think I was slow on the uptake. The snow has turned to slush.
I heard it. I understand it. That's enough.

He pours a drink, drinks.

You think I'm past my job, do you? You think I'm a bit slow?
Don't you believe it. I'm as quick as a python.

LUSH
An adder.

ROOTE
What?

LUSH

An adder.

ROOTE

What do you mean, an adder?

GIBBS

Do you think I deserve a little tipple of whisky, sir?

ROOTE

Good God, Gibbs is being jocular. Did you hear that, Lush? He's just made a pleasantry. Didn't you, son? Oh, that's better. I can feel a draught. See if you can turn that radiator off. If we can't turn it off here we'll have to get hold of Tubb and tell him to turn it off at the mains.

LUSH *bends to the radiator.*

Well?

LUSH

It won't budge. It's stiff.

ROOTE

It'll have to be turned off at the mains.

LUSH

It's a very cold building, sir, it's perishing on the upper floors.

ROOTE

I tell you it's too bloody hot and the damned heating's got to go off! Who's the boss here, for Christ's sake, you or me?

LUSH

Not me.

ROOTE

I do ten times as much work as the whole lot of you put
together. I deserve a bit of comfort, a bit of consideration.
The heating will have to be turned off! Every single pipe of it.
That's what causes the laxity, the skiving, the inefficiency in
this place. It's overheated! Always has been. (*To* GIBBS.)
What's the matter with you, standing there like a tit in a
trance? Tip the bottle, for the love of Mike. Deserved or
undeserved.

GIBBS *pours himself a glass of whisky.*

What do you mean, you deserve it, anyway? You deserve
nothing.

GIBBS

I meant for locating the father, sir.

ROOTE

You deserve nothing. Either of you. You've got a job to do.
Do it. You won't get any tulips from me. Come on, fill it up,
we'll drink a toast. Got yours, Lush?

LUSH

Just a minute.

LUSH *pours a glass of whisky.*

ROOTE (*solemnly*)

I'd like to drink a toast.

LUSH

To whom, sir?

ROOTE

I'd like to drink a toast, gentlemen, to our glorious dead.

LUSH

Which ones are they, sir?

ROOTE

The chaps who died for us in the field of action.

LUSH

Oh yes.

ROOTE

The men who gave their lives so that we might live. Who sacrificed themselves so that we might continue. Who helped keep the world clean for the generations to come. The men who died in our name. Let us drink to them. After all, it's Christmas. Couldn't be more appropriate.

LUSH

My glass is ready, sir.

ROOTE

Is yours ready, Gibbs?

GIBBS

It is.

ROOTE

Gentlemen, I give you a toast. To our glorious dead. (*Rising*.)

GIBBS *and* LUSH

To our glorious dead.

They drink.

ROOTE

A rapist on my own staff and I don't know what he looks like.
It's ridiculous. What sort of man is he?

GIBBS

Lamb, sir? Nondescript.

ROOTE

Tall?

GIBBS

No, sir. Small.

LUSH

Tall.

GIBBS

Small.

Pause

ROOTE

Do you know him, Lush?

LUSH

I've seen him.

ROOTE

Is he fat?

GIBBS

Thin, sir.

LUSH

Fat.

GIBBS

Thin.

Pause

ROOTE

Brown eyes?

GIBBS

Blue, sir.

LUSH

Brown.

GIBBS

Blue.

Pause

ROOTE

Curly hair?

GIBBS *and* LUSH *eye each other.*

LUSH

Straight, sir.

GIBBS

Curly.

LUSH

Straight.

Pause

ROOTE

What colour teeth?

GIBBS

Lemon, sir.

LUSH

Nigger.

GIBBS

Lemon.

LUSH

Nigger.

Pause

ROOTE

Any special peculiarities?

GIBBS

None.

LUSH

One.

GIBBS

None.

Pause

ROOTE

These descriptions don't tally. Next time bring me a photograph. Or you've got a cine-camera. You could devote a halfhour film to the man. A documentary – for educational purposes. It's still stifling in here. We'll have to get hold of Tubb. It's uncommonly warm in here for this time of the year, isn't it?

LUSH

It's warm out too. The snow has turned to slush.

ROOTE *turns, expostulating.*

GIBBS

Shall I call Tubb on the intercom, sir?

LUSH

I tried the intercom before. It sounded a bit clogged up.

ROOTE

Clogged up? What's the matter with this place? Everything's clogged up, bunged up, stuffed up, buggered up. The whole thing's running down hill. I don't like the look of it. Let's see.

He switches on the intercom on his desk and sits. A voice is heard.

VOICE

Number 84. A duck. Who's got ticket number 84? A duck ready for the oven. No-one? Unclaimed, Fred. Next one coming up. Ticket number 21. Number 21. Ten Portuguese cigars. Ten beautiful Portuguese cigars. No-one? Unclaimed, Fred. Number 38. Two tickets to the circus. Two tickets to the circus. Unclaimed, Fred. Number 44. A lovely crockery, cutlery, china and cookery set. A lovely crockery, cutlery, china and cookery set. Number 44. Unclaimed, Fred.

ROOTE *switches off.*

ROOTE

Yes, it does sound a bit clogged up, I must admit.

He fills the glasses.

What's it all about?

LUSH

It's the Christmas raffle, held by the understaff in the understaff canteen.

ROOTE

Raffle? Did we get any tickets?

GIBBS

I was approached, sir, but on behalf of the staff declined to purchase any.

ROOTE

Did you? Well, there's a bloody big amount of unclaimed stuff down there, isn't there?

LUSH

Must be a whole pile of it.

ROOTE

Well, who gets it?

LUSH

I expect there'll be another raffle at Easter, sir.

ROOTE

What about that duck? You can't keep a duck until Easter!
It's . . . it's just not sensible! There's not much I don't know
about poultry. Lush, make an immediate inquiry as to what's
to become of that duck.
He sits.

LUSH

Yes, sir. What about the two tickets to the circus?

ROOTE

Christmas, eh? And I haven't received one present. Not one
gift, of any kind. It's most upsetting.

LUSH

Actually, I've seen the duck, sir.

ROOTE

You have? What's it like?

LUSH

It's a dead duck, sir.

ROOTE

Dead?

LUSH

Quite dead, sir.

ROOTE

Good God, I didn't know it was dead.

LUSH

Yes, as dead as patient 6457. If not deader.

Silence

GIBBS

Is this Ministry whisky, sir? It's quite excellent.

ROOTE (*to* LUSH)

What do you know about 6457?

GIBBS

I wouldn't advise any further discussion of that matter, sir.

ROOTE

What do you know about 6457?

LUSH

I know that he's dead.

ROOTE

What do you know about it?

GIBBS

It is inadvisable to discuss the matter any further, sir.

ROOTE (*to* LUSH)

You're damned clever, aren't you?

LUSH

As a matter of fact, I met a relation of 6457's today.

ROOTE

You what?

GIBBS

Lush. The matter is closed.

ROOTE

What relation?

LUSH

His mother.

ROOTE

How do you know she was his mother?

LUSH

She said so.

ROOTE

She was a liar!

LUSH

No, she wasn't.

ROOTE

How do you know?

LUSH

She looked like a mother.

ROOTE

How do you know what mothers look like?

LUSH

I had one myself.

ROOTE

Do you think I didn't?

LUSH (*pointing at* GIBBS)

He didn't.

GIBBS

Oh yes, I did, damn you!

ROOTE

I was fed, Mister Cleverboots, at my mother's breast.

GIBBS

So was I.

LUSH

Me too.

Sudden silence

ROOTE
WELL? AND WHAT ABOUT IT?

ROOTE *sinks back in his seat. He looks at his glass, picks it up and swallows the glassful. He chokes, stands, writhes about in a fit of coughing.* GIBBS *and* LUSH *go to his aid.*

GIBBS (*taking his left arm*)
Come and sit in the armchair, sir.

LUSH (*taking his right arm*)
Come and sit on the sofa, sir.

A short tug-of-war commences, ROOTE *still coughing.*

ROOTE *shakes them off. He stands, shaking and panting.*

LUSH *goes to the desk, picks up a glass of whisky, takes it to* ROOTE.

LUSH

Here, drink this, sir.

ROOTE *viciously knocks the glass out of his hand. He stands, glaring at them, then goes back to his desk, sits.* LUSH *picks up the glass and places it on* ROOTE's *desk.* LUSH *fills his glass.*

ROOTE

6457's mother, eh? How did she get in? Wasn't the porter on duty at the gate?

LUSH

Don't you want to know what she wanted?

ROOTE

I want to know why the porter wasn't on duty at the gate!

GIBBS

He's in charge of the raffle, sir, in the understaff canteen.

ROOTE

Tubb? That was Tubb just now, on the intercom?

LUSH

Oh, very much Tubb, sir.

ROOTE

Holding a raffle when he should have been on duty at the gate? Honestly, things are going from bad to worse. (*Pouring.*) Down the hatch. (*He raises his glass.*)

GIBBS

Happy Christmas, sir.

ROOTE

Happy Christmas to you, Gibbs.

LUSH

Happy Christmas, sir.

ROOTE

Thank you. Happy Christmas to you, Lush. A happy Christmas to you both.

GIBBS *and* **LUSH** (*raising their glasses*)

And to you, sir.

ROOTE

Thanks. And the best of luck for the new year.

GIBBS *and* **LUSH**

The best of luck for the new year to you, sir.

A knock at the door.

ROOTE

Who's that?

TUBB

Tubb, sir.

ROOTE

Come in.

Enter TUBB, *carrying a small box.*

Tubb! I thought you were on the intercom.

TUBB

Merry Christmas to you, Colonel.

ROOTE

Thank you, Tubb. And to you.

TUBB

How did you enjoy your Christmas dinner, sir?

ROOTE

Disappointing.

TUBB

Oh, I'm sorry to hear that, Colonel.

ROOTE

Too much gravy.

LUSH

Really? Mine was bone dry.

ROOTE

What?

LUSH

Honestly. Bone dry.

ROOTE

Well, mine was swimming in gravy.

LUSH

That's funny, isn't it, Gibbs? His was swimming in gravy and
mine was bone dry.

TUBB

I'm surprised to hear yours was wet, Colonel.

ROOTE

Well, it was. Very wet.

He looks at the box.

What have you got there, Tubb?

TUBB

It's a Christmas present for you, Colonel.

ROOTE

A present?

TUBB

Just a little token of the understaff's regard, Colonel. Just a little something for Christmas.

ROOTE

Not a duck, by any chance?

TUBB

A duck, Colonel?

ROOTE

I just wondered whether it might have been a duck.

TUBB

Oh no, we haven't got any duck, sir.

ROOTE

No duck?

TUBB

No, sir.

ROOTE

What about number 84 then? Eh? Unclaimed. Ready for the oven. What? That was a duck wasn't it? And what's more it was unclaimed.

TUBB

Oh, that duck. Oh, that was claimed.

ROOTE (*startled*)

Claimed? Who by?

TUBB

Well, it wasn't exactly claimed, sir. But we found out who owned the ticket, so we're keeping it for him till he turns up, it's only fair.

ROOTE

Who is it?

TUBB

A man called Lamb, sir.

Silence

But anyway, what I've got here, Colonel, is a little token of regard from the understaff and the compliments of the season from all of us in the understaff, wishing you all the very best of luck in the year to come.

ROOTE

Thanks very much, Tubb. What is it?

TUBB

It's a Christmas cake, Colonel, cooked by the cook.

ROOTE

A cake? For me?

LUSH

That's very nice, isn't it, Gibbs?

ROOTE

A cake? For me?

TUBB

For you, sir.

ROOTE

How kind. How very kind. I'm most touched. Most touched. More than touched. Deeply moved. It's a long time, a very long time, since I had a Christmas cake. A long long time.

Pause

This ... was from the cook?

TUBB

From the cook, sir, from me, sir, from the kitchen staff, sir, from the portering staff, sir, from the cleaning staff, sir, from the very whole of the understaff, sir, from the very all of us ... to you, sir.

ROOTE

How very kind. How very very kind. I'm deeply moved. Deeply moved. More than moved ...

LUSH

What an awfully nice gesture.

TUBB

The understaff, Colonel, and I'm sure the patients, would be even more deeply moved if you were to give them a Christmas address, sir.

ROOTE

An address?

TUBB

They would be most touched, sir. They're all clustered up now in the canteen and I've fitted up the loudspeaker system with an extension to all the corridors leading onto the patients' rooms as well.

LUSH

What a splendid idea.

ROOTE

An address? Your people would appreciate an address, would they?

TUBB

Oh, they would, sir. I know they would. Just a little word for Christmas.

LUSH

What an exciting innovation.

ROOTE

And the patients ... they haven't expressed any desire ... themselves ... have they?

TUBB

Well, not exactly expressed one, sir, as far as I know, but I've fitted up the loudspeaker system to their rooms and I'm sure they'd be deeply moved.

Pause

ROOTE

What do you think, Gibbs?

Pause

Gibbs!

GIBBS

I beg pardon, sir?

ROOTE

I said what do you think?

GIBBS

I ... I think it's an excellent idea, sir.

ROOTE

Lush?

LUSH

I think it would be deeply moving, sir.

Pause

ROOTE (*briskly*)

Where's the mike?

TUBB

In the cake, sir.

ROOTE

In the cake!

TUBB

I just shoved it in with the cake, sir.

ROOTE

Well, it's got no business to be anywhere near the cake!
What's the matter with you? (*Muttering.*) What a place to put
a mike!

TUBB (*extracting mike*)

Here we are, Colonel.

ROOTE

Well, plug it in, let's get on with it.

TUBB *plugs in by the wall.* ROOTE *sits, clears his throat.*

TUBB (*with mike*)

On here on the blotting paper all right, sir?

ROOTE

Move out of it.

TUBB

Switch this switch when you're ready, Colonel.

ROOTE (*slowly*)

Yes.

TUBB

They're all ready. They're all clustered up in the understaff canteen.

Pause

ROOTE

What are you looking at, Gibbs?

GIBBS

Nothing in particular, sir.

ROOTE

You were looking at me! Do you call that nothing in particular?

Pause

I can't do it now. I'll do it later on. Later on. You can't make a speech like that without some thought. Tell them not to be disappointed. Tell them they'll hear my Christmas address later on. Later on.

The lights go down on the office. They go up on the sitting room.
MISS CUTTS *comes in. She sits, takes a table tennis ball from her pocket, tosses it up and catches it.*
GIBBS *descends the stairs.*
Suddenly a long sigh is heard, amplified.
GIBBS *stops.* MISS CUTTS *, about to toss the ball, stops.*
A long keen is heard, amplified.
GIBBS *looks up.* MISS CUTTS *looks up.*
A laugh is heard, amplified, dying away.
Silence.

MISS CUTTS *puts the ball to her mouth.*
GIBBS *is still a moment, then turns and enters the sitting room.*
MISS CUTTS *throws the ball at him. It falls at his feet.*

CUTTS

Catch!

GIBBS *looks down at the ball and stamps on it.*

GIBBS

Don't do that.

He takes out a packet of pills and swallows one.

CUTTS

What's the matter, Charlie?

GIBBS

Headache.

He sits, closes his eyes.
MISS CUTTS *goes to him.*

CUTTS

Have you got a headache, darling? Come to room 1A. (*She kisses him.*) I'll make it better for you. Are you coming?

GIBBS

I've got to go back.

CUTTS

What! Why?

GIBBS

To hear his Christmas address.

CUTTS

Another one? Oh, God, I thought he'd forgotten all about it.

GIBBS

He hadn't forgotten.

CUTTS

Every year. Sometimes I could scream.

GIBBS

I can't stand screaming.

CUTTS

Charlie, what is it? Don't I please you any more? Tell me. Be honest. Am I no longer the pleasure I was? Be frank with me. Am I failing you?

GIBBS

Stop it. I'm not in the mood.

CUTTS

Let me massage your neck.

She touches his neck.

GIBBS (*throwing her off*)

You and your necks! You love to get your hands round someone's neck!

CUTTS

So do you.

GIBBS

I'm not in the habit of touching people's necks.

CUTTS

It was such fun working with you this morning.

She sits.

You're so clever. I think you're the cleverest man I've ever had anything to do with. We don't work together nearly enough. It's such fun in room 1A. I think that's my favourite room in the whole place. It's such an intimate room. You can ask the questions and be so intimate. I love your questions. They're so intimate themselves. That's what makes it so exciting. The intimacy becomes unbearable. You keep waiting for the questions to stop, to pass from one intimacy into another, beautifully, and just when you know you can't ask another one, that they must stop, that you must stop, that it must stop — they stop! — and we're alone, and we can start, we can continue, in room 1A, because you know, you always know, your sense of timing is perfect, you know when the questions must stop, *those* questions, and you must start asking me questions, other questions, and I must start asking you questions, and it's question time, question time, question time, forever and forever and forever.

GIBBS (*standing*)

I tell you I'm not in the mood.

CUTTS

Come to 1A, Charlie.

GIBBS *stands, looking at the door.*

GIBBS

Did you hear anything, just now?

CUTTS

What?

GIBBS

Something. Sounds. Sounds. Just now. Just before.

CUTTS

Nothing. Not a thing. Nothing.

She looks at him.

What was it?

GIBBS

I don't know.

CUTTS (*a nervous chuckle*)

Don't tell me something's going to happen?

GIBBS

Something's *happening*. But I don't know what. I can't ...
define it.

CUTTS

How absurd.

GIBBS

It is absurd. Something's happening, I feel it, I know it, and I can't define it. It's ... it's ridiculous.

CUTTS

I know what's going to happen.

GIBBS

That old fool in there, he sees nothing, getting drunk with that ... bitch.

CUTTS

I know what's going to happen. You're going to kill him.

GIBBS

What?

CUTTS

Aren't you? You promised. You promised you would. Didn't you? Do it now. Now. Before he makes his Christmas speech.

GIBBS

Oh, stow it, for God's sake!

CUTTS

But you said you would!

GIBBS

Did I?

CUTTS

You said you'd stab him and pretend it was someone else.

GIBBS

Really? Who?

CUTTS

Lush.

GIBBS

Lush? Lush could never be taken for a murderer. He's scum but he's not a murderer.

CUTTS

No, but you are.

GIBBS *stares at her.*

GIBBS (*quietly*)

What did you say?

Pause

What did you call me?

CUTTS

Nothing.

GIBBS

You called me a murderer.

CUTTS

No, I didn't call you anything –

GIBBS (*ice*)

How dare you call me a murderer?

CUTTS

But I didn't!

GIBBS

Who do you know that I've murdered?

CUTTS

No-one!

GIBBS

Then how dare you call me a murderer?

CUTTS

You're not a murderer!

GIBBS (*hissing*)

I'm not a murderer, he's a murderer, Roote is a murderer!

Pause

You dare to call me a murderer?

CUTTS (*moaning*)

No, Charlie.

GIBBS

You know what that is, don't you? Slander. Defamation of character.

Pause

And on top of that, you try to incite me to kill my chief, Mr Roote. The man in charge. You, his own mistress. Just to satisfy your own personal whim.

Pause

CUTTS

Charlie . . .

GIBBS

Shut up!

MISS CUTTS *falls out of her chair onto the floor.*

CUTTS (*whispering*)

Oh, I wish I was in room 1A. I shall never get to room 1A again. I know I won't. Ever.

Blackout.
A drone is heard.
The drone stops.
Lights go up on the office.
ROOTE *and* LUSH *are still drinking.*
ROOTE *is at the desk,* LUSH *is seated, drooping.*
ROOTE *rises and perches on the front of the desk.*

ROOTE

Women! I've known them all. Did I ever tell you about the woman in the blue dress? She was a spy. A spy in a blue dress. I met her in Casablanca. Believe it or believe it not that woman was an agent for a foreign power. She was tattooed on her belly with a pelican. Yes. Her belly was covered with a pelican. She could make that pelican waddle across the room to you. On all fours, sideways, feet first, arse-upwards, any way you like. Her control was superhuman. Only a woman could possess it. Under her blue dress she wore a shimmy. And under that shimmy she wore a pelican.

Pause

My cake! We haven't cut the cake! My God, and it's nearly midnight.

He unwraps the cake, holds it.

A beauty. (*Going to his desk drawer.*) Wait a minute. Where are we? Just the thing in here.

Takes a bayonet from the drawer.

Now. Right down the middle.

He cuts the cake.

I remember the day my walls used to be hung with Christmas cards, I used to walk knee deep in presents, all my aunties and uncles popping in for a drink, a log fire in the grate, bells on the Christmas tree, garlands, flowers, floral decoration, music, flowers ... floral decoration ... laughter ... (*Abruptly.*) I didn't notice a card from you, did I? Didn't expect it either. Because you've no sense of decorum, it sticks out a mile. No heart. It's not so much the language, it's the attitude of mind that's nasty, unwholesome, putrid.

LUSH

The snow has turned to slush.

ROOTE

The temperature must have dropped. (*Thrusting a piece of cake at him.*) Well, here you are, have a piece of this cake.

LUSH *stares at it.*

Go on. Eat it!

They both munch. LUSH *spits his out.* ROOTE *grabs him by the neck.*

What are you doing? That's my cake!

LUSH
I can't!

ROOTE (*shaking him*)
That's my Christmas cake! You can't spit out my Christmas cake!

LUSH (*violently, breaking away*)
Stuff it!

ROOTE *regards him.*

ROOTE (*gravely*)
You've insulted me, you've insulted the cook, and you've insulted Jesus Christ.

Pause

We've got no room for unhealthy minds in this establishment.

LUSH (*muttering*)
Muck and slush.

ROOTE
Lush!

LUSH
Colonel?

ROOTE (*grimly*)

I said you'd better watch your step. Everyone had better watch their step! (*He begins to move about the room.*) I don't like the look of things. You can't trust a soul. And there's something going on here that I haven't quite cottoned on to. There's something funny afoot. I can feel it. Some people think I'm old, but oh no, not by a long chalk. I've got second sight. I can see through walls. (*He considers.*) I don't mean that that's second sight, seeing through walls. I mean I've got second sight *and* I can see through walls!

LUSH

And your knowledge of phytotomy, sir.

ROOTE

That's more than a passing acquaintance. I can see right through them. I can hear a whisper in the basement. I didn't waste my youth. I exercised my faculties – to the hilt! And I spent a lot of time pondering. Pondering. For instance, this stupid business of the world going round. It's all a lot of balls. If the world was going round we'd be falling about all over the room. (*Bending over* LUSH.) But are we? Are we?

LUSH *considers.*

And today I feel something in my bones. I know it. Something's going on which I can't define. It's ridiculous. But I don't damn well know what it is. Do you think I'm going to be murdered?

LUSH

That's it.

ROOTE *brings the bottle to the desk and pours.*

The day got off to a lousy start! A death and a birth. Absolutely bloody scandalous! Is it too much to ask — to keep the place clean?

LUSH *goes to the desk, pours a drink, goes back to the armchair.*

You know who you remind me of? You remind me of Whipper Wallace, back in the good old days.

The door opens. GIBBS *enters and stands still.*

He used to hang about with a chap called House-Peters. Boghouse-Peters we used to call him. I remember one day the Whipper and Boghouse — he had a scar on his left cheek, Boghouse — caught in some boghouse brawl, I suppose. (*He laughs.*) Well, anyway, there they were, the Whipper and Boghouse, rolling down the banks of the Euphrates this night, when up came a policeman . . .

He dissolves in laughter.

up came this policeman . . . up came a policeman . . . this policeman . . . approached . . . Boghouse . . . and the Whipper . . . were questioned . . . this night . . . the Euphrates . . . a policeman . . .

GIBBS *moves.* ROOTE *jumps.*

Aaaaahhhh! (*To him.*) What the bloody hell do you think you're doing, creeping up behind me like a snake! Eh? You frightened the life out of me.

GIBBS

I've come to hear the Christmas speech, sir.

ROOTE

Well, why don't you make it? You're dying to make it, aren't you? Why don't you make it?

GIBBS

It's your privilege, sir.

ROOTE

Well, I'm sick to death of it! The patients, the staff, the understaff, the whole damn thing!

GIBBS

I'm sorry to hear that, sir.

ROOTE

It's bleeding me to death.

LUSH

Then why do you continue?

ROOTE *looks at him.*

ROOTE

Because I'm a delegate.

LUSH

A delegate of what?

ROOTE *(calmly)*

I tell you I'm a delegate.

LUSH

A delegate of what?

They stare at each other.

ROOTE

Not only me. All of us. That bastard there. (*To* GIBBS.)
Aren't you?

GIBBS

I am.

ROOTE

There you are.

LUSH

You haven't explained yourself.

ROOTE

Who hasn't?

LUSH

You can't explain yourself.

ROOTE

I can't?

LUSH

Explain yourself.

GIBBS

He's drunk.

ROOTE (*moving to him*)

Explain yourself, Lush.

LUSH

No, you! You explain yourself!

ROOTE

Be careful, sonny.

LUSH (*rising*)

You're a delegate, are you?

ROOTE (*facing him squarely*)

I am.

LUSH

On whose authority? With what power are you entrusted? By whom were you appointed? Of *what* are you a delegate?

ROOTE *hits him in the stomach.*

ROOTE

I'm a delegate! (*He hits him in the stomach.*)
I was entrusted! (*He hits him in the stomach.*)
I'm a delegate! (*He hits him in the stomach.*)
I was appointed!

LUSH *backs, crouched, slowly across the stage,* ROOTE *following him.*

Delegated! (*He hits him in the stomach.*)
Appointed! (*He hits him in the stomach.*)
Entrusted!

He hits him in the stomach. LUSH *sinks to the floor.*
ROOTE *stands over him and shouts:*

I AM AUTHORISED!

LUSH *remains heaped on the floor.* ROOTE *goes back to the desk, pours a drink for himself and* GIBBS.

ROOTE (*to* GIBBS, *sourly*)
What do you want?

GIBBS
I came to hear your Christmas speech, Colonel.

ROOTE
You're sure you didn't come here to murder me?

GIBBS
Murder you?

ROOTE
Yes, wasn't that why you came?

GIBBS
Certainly not. What an idea.

ROOTE
Yes, you did! I can see it in your eyes! Can you see it, Lush, in his eyes? This chap came here to do me in. You can see it in his eyes.

GIBBS
I did no such thing.

ROOTE

You went cross-eyed, man, don't argue with me. Guilty! It was written all over your face.

GIBBS

This is ridiculous.

ROOTE

Yes, well, you're not much good at it, are you? You're pretty poor at it. I twigged it like that! (*He clicks his fingers, laughs.*) Didn't I? You won't get very far as a murderer, will he, Lush?

LUSH *begins to stand, slowly.*

Will you?

GIBBS

I resent this levity, sir.

ROOTE

Do you?

GIBBS

I resent it very strongly.

ROOTE

He resents it. (*Going behind the desk with his drink.*) Well, if he resents it he resents it. (*Drinks.*) You're just too sensitive, that's your trouble.

GIBBS (*sitting*)

A foul insinuation.

ROOTE

Oh, don't be so touchy!

LUSH *walks carefully to* GIBBS.

LUSH

He was only having a little joke, Gibbs old man.

ROOTE

Of course I was.

GIBBS

I found it less than funny.

LUSH

He didn't mean it. Honestly. Don't be downhearted. Now give me the knife and we won't say another word.

Sudden silence.
All still. GIBBS *and* LUSH *stare at each other.*
LUSH *makes a tiny movement to his jacket.*
Immediately GIBBS *rises, with a knife in his hand.*
LUSH *faces him, a knife in his hand.*
ROOTE *seizes the bayonet from his desk, comes above them, covering them both, grinning.*
Silence. All knives up.
Suddenly a long sigh is heard, amplified.
The knives go down.
A long keen is heard, amplified.
They look up.
A laugh is heard, amplified, dying away.
Silence.

LUSH

What was that?

ROOTE

I don't know. What was it?

GIBBS

I don't know.

Pause

ROOTE

I heard something, didn't you?

LUSH

Yes, I did.

GIBBS

Yes, I heard something.

Pause

ROOTE

Well, what was it?

Pause

GIBBS

I don't know.

LUSH

Nor do I.

Pause

ROOTE

Well, is there any way of finding out?

GIBBS

Something's happening, sir. I don't like it. There's something going on ... which I can't quite define.

ROOTE

How odd you should say that. I was only saying the same before, wasn't I, Lush? I was saying the same before. Just before you came in.

Pause

GIBBS

We'll investigate. Come on, Lush.

LUSH

Go yourself.

ROOTE

Go with him.

LUSH

I don't want to go with him.

ROOTE

Go with him! What's the matter? Are you frightened of the dark?

LUSH (*shyly*)

No ... well, you see, the fact is, Colonel, I've ... I've got a present for you.

ROOTE

A present?

LUSH

A Christmas present.

ROOTE (*suspiciously*)

Oh yes? What sort of a present?

LUSH

Just a little something, sir, for Christmas.

He takes a cigar from his pocket and hands it to ROOTE.

This is it.

ROOTE

I say! That looks a fine one.

LUSH

Just a little token, sir.

ROOTE

Well, that's a very nice thought, Lush my lad. I'm deeply
gratified.

LUSH

I'm glad you like it, sir.

ROOTE (*beaming*)

Yes, very nice. I shall smoke it before I go to bed. Now off
you go, about your business.

GIBBS

When would you like to see Lamb, sir?

ROOTE

Lamb?

GIBBS

The father, sir.

ROOTE

Oh, him. In the morning, son, in the morning. I can't be bothered to bother with him now. Can I?

GIBBS

In the morning then. Thank you for the drink, sir.

LUSH

And the cake.

ROOTE

Goodnight, gentlemen.

GIBBS *and* LUSH *go out.*
ROOTE *walks, with the cigar, to the sofa.*
MISS CUTTS *appears behind him from the bedroom door, watches him. She wears a nightdress.*
ROOTE *lights the cigar, puffs.*
The cigar explodes.
MISS CUTTS *rushes to him.* ROOTE *throws the cigar down, sees* MISS CUTTS.

CUTTS

Are you all right?

ROOTE *stares at her.*

What's the matter with that cigar?

ROOTE

You remind me of someone.

CUTTS

In my new nightie? Who?

ROOTE

Where did you get that thing?

CUTTS

It's a gift. Who do I remind you of?

ROOTE

Where did you get it?

CUTTS

From a friend. Do you like it? She just gave it to me. I had tea with her today. She's a nursing mother. She doesn't need it. She insisted I should have it. She's so sweet, and she's got such a bonny baby. I said to her, now we're friends, I can't go on calling you 6459, can I? What's your name? Do you know, she wouldn't tell me? Well, what does your lover call you? I said, what little nickname? She blushed to the roots of her hair. I must say I'm very curious. What could he have called her? She's sweet, but she said the baby misses his Daddy. Babies do miss Daddy, you know. Archie, can't the baby see his Daddy, just for a little while, just to say hello?

ROOTE (*quietly*)

No. Daddy will stay where he is.

CUTTS

Where is he?

ROOTE

You're supposed to be on nightshift.

CUTTS

Oh, it's Christmas, I knocked off early.

ROOTE

You're supposed to be working.

CUTTS

You're not pleased to see me.

Pause. ROOTE *sighs, looks at her.*

ROOTE

Are you ...

He sits on the sofa with her.

Are you ... happy?

CUTTS

Happy? Of course I am.

ROOTE

Are you ... are you happy with me?

CUTTS

Of course I'm happy. With you. When you're not silly.

ROOTE

You're really happy with me?

CUTTS

Not when you want me to go out into the cold with my nightie on.

ROOTE (*taking her hand*)

Don't go out.

He caresses her hand. She regards him gravely.

CUTTS

You know, sometimes I think I'm not feminine enough for you.

ROOTE

You are, you are feminine enough for me.

CUTTS

Perhaps if I was more feminine you wouldn't want me to go out in the cold.

ROOTE

I don't want you to go out. I want you to stay.

CUTTS

Or perhaps ... perhaps it's because you think you're not masculine enough.

ROOTE

I am!

CUTTS

Perhaps you're not.

ROOTE

You can't want me to be *more* masculine?

CUTTS (*urgently*)

It's not what *I* want. It's what *you* really *think*. It's what you really *deeply* think and *feel*. It's what *you* want, it's what you truly *are*, can't you see that, Archie? I mean, if you're suddenly worried that you're not masculine enough – I mean, that I'm not feminine enough and that you're too feminine – well, it's not going to work, is it?

ROOTE

Now, wait a minute, I never said anything–

CUTTS (*intensely*)

If I didn't love you so much it wouldn't matter. Do you remember the first time we met? On the beach? In the night? All those people? And the bonfire? And the waves? And the spray? And the mist? And the moon? Everyone dancing, somersaulting, laughing? And you – standing silent, staring at a sandcastle in your sheer white trunks. The moon was behind you, in front of you, all over you, suffusing you, consuming you, you were transparent, translucent, a beacon. I was struck dumb, dumbstruck. Water rose up my legs. I could not move. I was rigid. Immovable. Our eyes met. Love at first sight. I held your gaze. And in your eyes, bold and unashamed, was desire. Brutal, demanding desire. Bestial, ruthless, remorseless. I stood there magnetised, hypnotised. Transfixed. Motionless and still. A spider caught in a web.

ROOTE *stands, goes to the desk, sits, switches on the microphone.*

ROOTE (*into the mike*)

Patients, staff and understaff. A merry Christmas to you all, and a happy and prosperous new year. And on behalf of all the staff I'd like to wish all the understaff the very best of luck for the year to come and a very happy Christmas. And to the patients I should like to send a personal greeting, to each and every one of them, wishing them the heartiest compliments of the season, and very best wishes, on behalf of the staff, the understaff and myself, not forgetting the Ministry, which I know would be glad to be associated with these words, for a healthy, happy and prosperous new year.

Pause

We have had our little difficulties, in the year that is about to die, our little troubles, our little sorrows as well as our little joys, but through working together, through each and every one of us pulling his weight, no matter how lowly or apparently trivial his job, by working, by living, by pulling together as one great family, we stand undaunted.

Pause

We say goodbye to the old year very soon now, and hail the new, but I say to you, as we stand before these embers, that we carry with us from the old year ... things ... which will stand us in good stead in the new, and we are not daunted.

Pause

Some of you, sitting at your loudspeakers tonight, may sometimes find yourselves wondering whether the little daily hardships, the little daily disappointments, the trials and tribulations which seem continually to dog you are, in the end, worth it. To you I would say one simple thing. Have faith.

Pause

Yes, I think if I were asked to convey to you a special message
this Christmas it would be that: Have faith.

Pause

Remember that you are not alone, that we here, for example,
in this our home, are inextricably related, one to another, the
staff to the understaff, the understaff to the patients, the
patients to the staff. Remember this, as you sit by your fires,
with your families, who have come from near and from far, to
share this day with you, and may you be content.

He switches off the microphone and sits.
The lights go down on the office.
Darkness.
A low light on the stairway and the forestage.
Squeaks are heard, of locks turning.
The rattle of chains.
A great clanging, reverberating, as of iron doors opening.
Shafts of light appear abruptly about the stage, as of doors open-
ing into corridors and into rooms.
Whispers, chuckles, half-screams of the patients grow.
The clanging of locks and doors grows in intensity.
The lights shift from area to area, rapidly.
The sounds reach a feverish pitch and stop.
Lights up on the office in the ministry.
LOBB *rises as* GIBBS *enters.*

LOBB

Ah, come in, Gibbs. How are you?

They shake hands.

Have a good journey down?

GIBBS

Not at all bad, thank you, sir.

LOBB

Sit down.

They sit.

LOBB

Cigarette?

GIBBS

No thank you, sir.

LOBB

You haven't been waiting long, have you?

GIBBS

Oh, no sir, not at all.

LOBB

My secretary's down with flu. Rather disorganised. What's the weather like up there?

GIBBS

Quite sharp, sir.

LOBB

Been fair to middling down here, for the time of year.
Treacherous, though. My secretary, for instance, quite a
stalwart sort of chap, strong as an ox, went down like a log
over the weekend.

GIBBS

It's certainly treacherous.

LOBB

Dreadful. How are you feeling yourself?

GIBBS

Oh, I'm quite fit, thank you, sir.

LOBB

Yes, you look fit. Remarkably fit, really. You wear a vest,
don't you?

GIBBS

Yes, sir.

LOBB

There you are. Very sensible. My secretary, for instance,
strong as an ox, but he never wore a vest in his life. That's
what did it.

Pause

Well, I'm glad you got down to see me, Gibbs.

GIBBS

So am I, sir.

LOBB

Rather unfortunate business. You've made out your report, I
take it?

GIBBS

Yes, sir.

LOBB

I haven't seen it yet.

GIBBS

No, sir. I have it with me.

LOBB

Hand it in to the office on the way out, will you?

GIBBS

Yes, sir.

LOBB

Got any definite figures?

GIBBS

Yes, I ... have, sir.

LOBB

What are they?

Pause

GIBBS

The whole staff was slaughtered, sir.

LOBB

The whole staff?

GIBBS

With one exception, of course.

LOBB

Who was that?

GIBBS

Me, sir.

LOBB

Oh yes, of course.

Pause

The whole staff, eh? A massacre, in fact?

GIBBS

Exactly.

LOBB

Most distressing.

Pause

How did they . . . how did they do it?

GIBBS

Various means, sir. Mr Roote and Miss Cutts were stabbed in their bed. Lush –

LOBB

Excuse me, did you say bed, or beds?

GIBB

Bed, sir.

LOBB

Oh, really? Yes, go on.

GIBBS

Lush, Hogg, Beck, Budd, Tuck, Dodds, Tate and Pett, sir, were hanged and strangled, variously.

LOBB

I see. Well, I should think there's going to be quite a few questions asked about this, Gibbs.

GIBBS

Yes, sir.

LOBB

What's the position now?

GIBBS

The patients are all back in their rooms. I've left the head porter, Tubb, in charge of things. He's very capable. All the understaff, of course, are still active.

LOBB

They didn't touch the understaff?

GIBBS

No. Just the staff.

LOBB

Ah. Look here, Gibbs, there's something I'd like to know. How did the patients get out?

GIBBS

I'm not sure that I can give an absolutely conclusive answer to that, sir, until the proper inquiry has been set in motion.

LOBB

Naturally, naturally.

GIBBS

One possibility though is that one of their doors may not have been properly locked, that the patient got out, filched the keys from the office, and let the others out.

LOBB

Good Lord.

GIBBS

You see, the locktester who should have been on duty – we always had a locktester on duty –

LOBB

Of course, of course.

GIBBS

Was absent from duty.

LOBB

Absent? I say, well . . . that's rather . . . significant, isn't it?

GIBBS

Yes, sir.

LOBB

What happened to him?

GIBBS

He's . . . not to be found, sir.

LOBB

Well, it would be a good thing if he were found, wouldn't it?

GIBBS

I shall do my best, sir.

LOBB

Good-o. (*Slight pause.*) Tell me. Why weren't you killed? Just as a matter of interest.

GIBBS

I was engaged on some research, sir, alone. I was probably the only member of the staff awake, so was able to take measures to protect myself.

LOBB

I see. Well, it's all most unfortunate, but we can't really do anything until the report has gone in and the inquiry set up. Meanwhile you'd better try to get hold of that locktester of yours. I think we shall probably want to have a word with him. What's his name?

GIBBS

Lamb, sir.

LOBB (*making a note of the name*)

Lamb. Well, Gibbs, I would like to say on behalf of the Ministry how very much we commend the guts you've shown.

GIBBS

Thank you, sir. My work means a great deal to me.

LOBB

That's the spirit. (*Slight pause.*) You can carry on now, I suppose? We'll have some reinforcements down in a few days. Can't be sooner, I'm afraid. We've got to get hold of some properly qualified people. Not as easy as all that.

GIBBS

I can carry on, sir.

LOBB

You'll be in charge, of course.

GIBBS

Thank you, sir.

LOBB (*rising*)

Don't thank me. It's we have to thank you.

They walk to the door.

One last question. Why do you think they did it? I mean . . . why did they feel so strongly?

GIBBS

Well, Mr. Lobb, it's a little delicate in my position . . .

LOBB

Go on, my boy, go on. It's the facts that count.

GIBBS

One doesn't like to speak ill of the dead.

LOBB

Naturally, naturally.

GIBBS

But there's no doubt that Mr Roote was unpopular.

LOBB

With good cause?

GIBBS

I'm afraid so, sir. Two things especially had made him rather unpopular. He had seduced patient 6459 and been the cause of her pregnancy, and he had murdered patient 6457. That had not gone down too well with the rest of the patients.

Blackout on office.

Lights rise on sound-proof room.

LAMB *in chair. He sits still, staring, as in a catatonic trance.*

Curtain.